FARTING !

ALL YOU WANTED TO KNOW ABOUT 'LETTING-ONE-RIP, BUT WERE AFRAID TO ASK...

by TONI GOFFE

FOR SOME IT IS...

First published in Great Britain by
Pendulum Gallery Press
56 Ackender Road, Alton, Hants GU34 1JS

© TONI GOFFE 1991

FARTING
ISBN 0-948912-17-0

REPRINTED 1989, 1990, 1991, 1992, 1993, 1994,
1995, 1997, 1998, 1999, 2001

PRINTED IN GREAT BRITAIN BY
UNWIN BROTHERS LTD. OLD WOKING, SURREY

DEDICATION: TO JOSEPH PUJOL – LE PETOMANE – WHOS LIFE OF FARTING
INSPIRED THIS FART TO WRITE THIS BOOK.

R·I·P·

WHERE EVER YOU
BE LET YOUR
WIND GO FREE
FOR KEEPING IT
IN WAS THE
DEATH
OF
ME

MY FATHER ALWAYS QUOTED THIS ANCIENT SAYING, EVERY TIME HE FARTED AT THE DINNER TABLE AND GOT A MEANINGFUL LOOK FROM MY MOTHER·

AS NOTHING ELSE HAPPENED, IT WAS LIKE A GREENLIGHT FOR ME· I REALISED THAT...

FARTING WAS OK !!...

IT THEN BECAME A CONTEST BETWEEN MY FATHER AND I, WHO COULD PRODUCE THE LOUDEST AND LONGEST FART AND ANNOY MY MOTHER THE MOST !

IT WAS A TURNING POINT IN MY LIFE.....

A BRIEF HISTORY: THE FIRST FART!

THE FART DID NOT HAVE A PROMISING START. IT PROBABLY PUT BACK THE DISCOVERY OF FIRE FOR, AT LEAST, A MILLION YEARS. SINCE THEN PEOPLE HAVE HELD THE FART IN A BAD LIGHT.

IT IS THE HOPE THAT THIS BOOK WILL BRING THE FART TO THE FOREFRONT OF HUMAN ENDEAVOUR, PUTTING IT IN IT'S PROPER PLACE IN THE AFFAIRS OF MEN.

'FOREWARD WITH THE FART!' IS THE CRY WE HOPE TO HEAR ECHOING DOWN THE STREETS OF OUR GREAT CITIES THE WORLD OVER. THE FART MUST BE BROUGHT OUT OF THE CLOSET.

EVERYONE SHOULD ENJOY FARTING AND NOT HOLD BACK, SECRETLY LETTING THEM OUT IN LITTLE 'PUFFS'.

LET YOUR FARTS GO! ENJOY THEM, SHARE THEM WITH YOUR FRIENDS. FARTERS OF THE WORLD UNITE!!

WHAT IS A FART?

THE DICTIONARY TELLS US THAT A FART IS...

N., & V. I. (INDECENT) EMISSION OF WIND FROM THE ANUS...

IS THAT ALL A FART IS!? OF COURSE NOT!! A FART IS A FRIEND! (I BET YOU HAVE MANY FRIENDS WHO ARE FARTS) IT CAN WARM YOU ON A COLD NIGHT (WAITING OUTSIDE YOUR GIRLFRIENDS HOUSE UNTIL HER HUSBAND GOES DOWN THE PUB) IT'S ALSO A FORM OF COMMUNICATION.. FART IN A CROWDED LIFT AND YOU'LL SOON HAVE SOMEONE TO TALK TO.

IT'S ALSO AN AID TO A BETTER RELATIONSHIP, PUT YOUR PARTNERS HAND ON YOUR BACKSIDE AS YOU FART INTO IT — NEW AREAS, OF YOUR RELATIONSHIP THAT YOU DIDN'T KNOW EXISTED WILL APPEAR IMMEDIATELY• A FART IS ALL THESE THINGS AND MUCH MORE — READ ON!

A **FART** IS WHAT HAPPENS TO THE STALE AIR IN YOUR STOMACH THAT HAS GONE DOWN TOO FAR TO COME BACK AS A BELCH!!...

HOW TO DO IT

10 PINTS OF LAGER FOLLOWED BY A VINDALOO CURRY.

THE POINT OF NO RETURN

ALTHOUGH FARTING IS CONSIDERED A MALE PRESERVE AS WELL AS A NATURAL PHENOMENON THERE ARE METHODS OF ENHANCING, WHAT AT FIRST IS A CONTROLLED EXHALATION OF HUMAN METHANE GAS THROUGH THE LOWER UNDERPANT, INTO A ROOM-SHATTERING EXPLOSION THAT COULD BRING PEOPLE OF THE STRONGEST PHYSIQUE TO THEIR KNEES....

...HERE ARE SOME WELL TRIED RECIPES....

... TRY DRINKING LEMONADE UPSIDE DOWN...

JUST OPEN YOUR MOUTH IN A HIGH WIND...

OR EAT SIX BOXES OF BRAN FOR BREAKFAST...

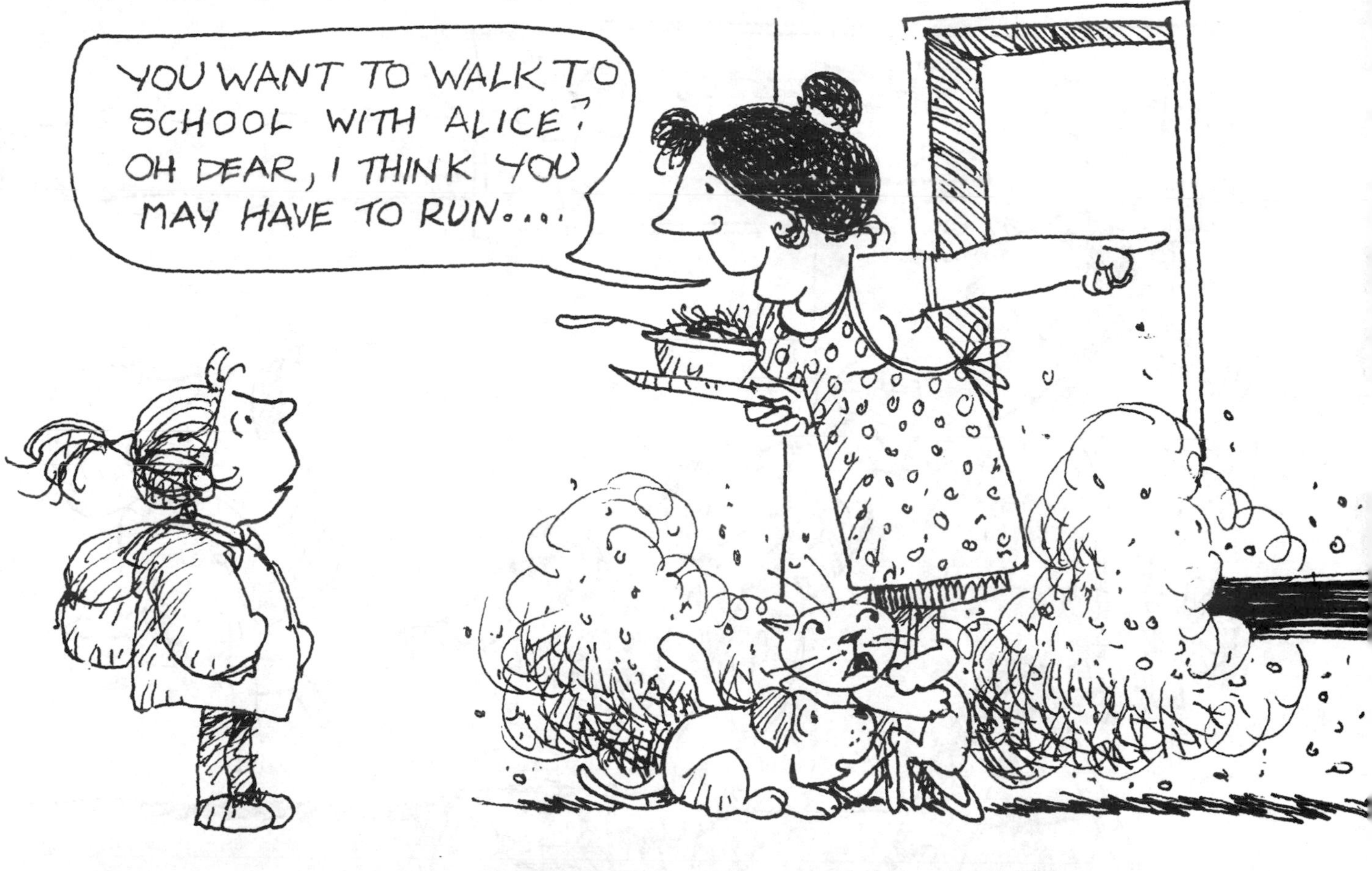

EAT OUT EVERY NIGHT IN FAST-FOOD RESTAURANTS....

HAVE A DINNER PARTY USING THE FOLLOWING...

WHEN YOU'VE TRIED ALL THOSE METHODS ... YOU MIGHT WANT TO TRY SOMETHING **DANGEROUS**!!! EAT MEXICAN FOODS! THEY CREATE **REALLY** HOT-FARTS. N·B· DON'T LET YOUR PETS STAND BEHIND YOU WHEN YOU EAT...

OH NO!! MY LITTLE BURRO- -IN-FURNACE!

N·B·(AGAIN) YOU MIGHT NEED SOME MEDICAL TREATMENT AFTERWARDS PARTICULARLY TO THE BURNT EDGES AREA OF YOUR LOWER UNDERPANT!

WHY DO WE FART?

FOR FUN OF COURSE, AND TO CAUSE AS MUCH EMBARRASSMENT AS POSSIBLE – AND GENERALLY TO CREATE <u>HAVOC</u>!

...HERE ARE SOME EXCUSES WE CAN USE IF WE'RE FOUND OUT................

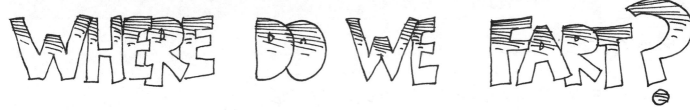

WHERE DO WE FART?

THE ANSWER IS ANYWHERE WHERE IT HAS THE MOST **EFFECT**!

IF YOU FEEL ONE COMING ON, SAVE IT UNTIL THE MOST DRAMATIC MOMENT...

...LIKE...

IN A LIFT...

AT A DINNER PARTY ....
AH! NOW THAT MEANS I REALLY ENJOYED THAT MEAL
I THOUGHT THAT WAS BELCHING?

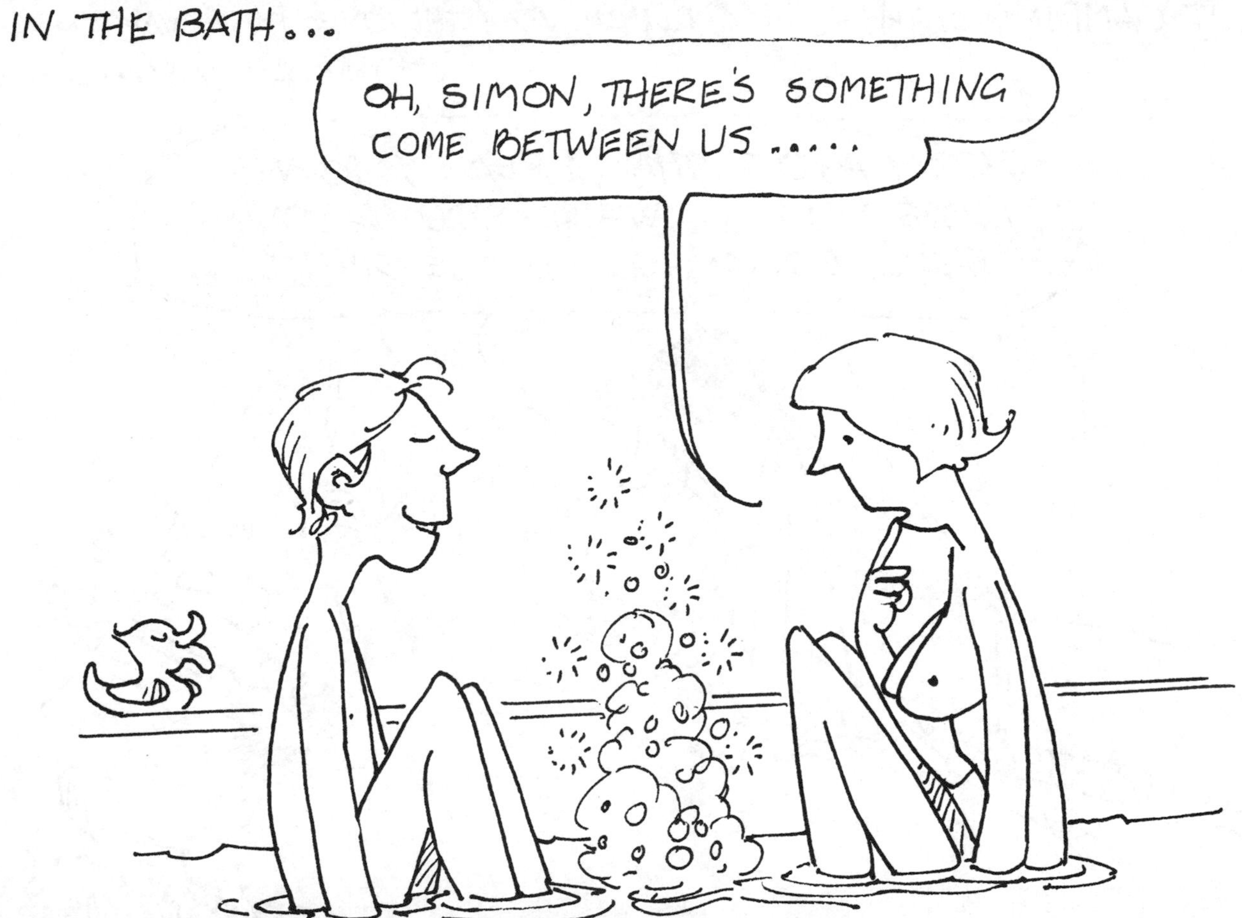
IN THE BATH...
OH, SIMON, THERE'S SOMETHING COME BETWEEN US .....

IN TRAIN CARRIAGES...

DURING THE RUSH·HOUR...

WHEN DO WE FART?

TIMING IS THE KEY WORD HERE. TO BE MOST
EFFECTIVE AND FUNNY AND ANNOYING, OF COURSE,...

... SO SAVE UP YOUR FARTS FOR ....

...WHEN EVERYONE IS ENJOYING A CONCERT AND THERE IS A DRAMATIC MUSICAL PAUSE....

... WHEN YOUR FAITHFUL TRUSTING DOG FORCES HIS HEAD BETWEEN YOUR LEGS AND LOOKS UP AT YOU FOR FOOD ...

... A LIFT JOURNEY. ONCE COMMITTED TO THE OUTSIDE OF YOUR BODY, BE SURE TO LOOK AT SOMEONE ELSE AS QUICKLY AS.
.. POSSIBLE!

THE SECRET FART

SECRET FARTING IS A BIT WIMPISH AND A SHAMEFUL WASTE OF A PRIME PRODUCT, BUT IT DOES HAVE ITS POINTS, LIKE BEING ABLE TO PUT THE BLAME ON SOMEONE OR SOMETHING ELSE.

THERE IS ALSO THE THEORY THAT WOMEN ARE SECRET FARTERS, BUT REALLY IT IS UNKNOWN IF WOMEN DO ACTUALLY FART. IF YOU ASK ONE, THEY USUALLY SAY "NO, THEY DON'T!" ONE OR TWO MAY ADMIT TO BREAKING-WIND, BUT THAT'S ... NOT **FARTING!** FOR THE TIME BEING IT WILL HAVE TO REMAIN A MYSTERY. FURTHER SURVEYS ARE CONTINUING AS I WRITE ....

HAVING FUN WITH FARTS

FARTING, AT IT'S BEST, SHOULD BE FUN. FUN FOR
EVERYONE. SHARE YOUR FARTING WITH YOUR FRIENDS.
SPREAD YOUR FARTS AROUND. FARTING IS SAFE, AND
MOST OF ALL, FARTING IS **FUN**!

SHARING, IS SUCH A WONDERFUL
EXPERIENCE WITH YOU SIMON...

HERE ARE SOME **FUN** THINGS TO DO
IN THE FARTING AREA............

TRY DEVELOPING YOUR BOTTOM MUSCLES AND LEARN TO SQUEEZE YOUR FARTS AS THEY COME OUT · THIS WILL PRODUCE AN INCREASINGLY HIGHER NOTE (LIKE A TRUMPET) WITH ASTONISHING EFFECTS....

TRY LIGHTING THEM:
AS FART GAS IS METHANE, IT CAN BE IGNITED WITH A MATCH. THIS, OF COURSE, COULD BE DANGEROUS — SO LET YOUR FRIENDS TRY IT FIRST — AND DON'T 'BREATHE' IN!

START A FART-CLUB:
FORM A BARBER-SHOP QUARTETTE, AND SEE
IF YOU CAN FART IN HARMONY.

... HOLD A FARTING CONTEST:
SEE WHO CAN MAKE THE LONGEST AND LOUDEST FART. HOLD IT IN YOUR LOCAL PUB OR IN THE BEST RESTAURANT IN TOWN.

BALLOON RACES:
FILL PAPER BAGS WITH HOT-FARTS AND SEE HOW FAR THEY'LL GO. ATTACH YOUR ADDRESS, YOU MIGHT MEET AN INTERESTING PEN-PAL.

AH! GOOD! SOMEONE WE COULD WRITE TO ON EARTH, WHERE EVER THAT IS!!

LEARN TO MAKE FART-TYPE NOISES WITH YOUR MOUTH OR ARM PIT · GREAT TO USE WHEN SOMEONE IS ABOUT TO SIT DOWN...

FUN WITH FOOD:
    FIRST, INVITE A FRIEND TO DINNER, ONE WHO WOULD BE MOST EMBARRASSED TO BE CAUGHT FARTING....
    MAKE A SAUCE FROM THE FOLLOWING: BAKED BEANS, SPLIT-PEAS. HÂRICOT BEANS, RED BEANS, LIMA BEANS, PARSNIPS, ARTICHOKES, RADISHES, LENTILS, BRUSSEL SPROUTS, CABBAGE AND HOT PEPPERS. COOK AND BLEND INTO A SAUCE AND POUR LIBERALLY ON TO WHAT YOU HAVE PREPARED FOR YOUR DINNER COMPANION AND SIT BACK AND WATCH OR EVEN BETTER TAKE THEM OUT TO SOME HEAVY SOCIAL SCENE. ENDLESS HOURS OF FUN HERE....

WELL, WHAT DO YOU THINK OF IT SO FAR?

TYPES OF FARTS

IF YOU'RE A CONNOISSEUR OF FARTING, LIKE A WINE CONNOISSEUR, YOU SHOULD BE ABLE TO TELL THE COUNTRY, REGION, VALLEY AND VINEYARD OF YOUR FART....

AH! THE TAJ MAHAL, LITTLE SNODDINGTON, HAMPSHIRE, ENGLAND, PRAWN MADRAS WITH BRINJAL PICKLE AND A PINT OF LAGER!

TWENTY PINTS OF LAGER!!

THE ANTI-VET FART:

THE VERY DANGEROUS... YOGA PLOUGH FART!

THE LOTUS POSITION - KNOTTED FART

THE SILENT-BUT-DEADLY FART...
USUALLY BY MANS BEST 'FRIEND' THE DOG!

BACKEND OF THE EPILOGUE:

WELL, THAT'S ALL FOR THE MOMENT ON 'FARTING'. ALL YOU WANTED TO KNOW ABOUT 'PUSHING-OUT-THE-METHANE' BUT WERE AFRAID TO ASK:

IF YOU <u>ARE</u> A FARTER, I HOPE THIS BOOK WILL HELP YOU BECOME A BIGGER AND BETTER FARTER:

IF YOU ARE <u>NOT</u> A FARTER, THEN THIS IS YOUR ONE AND ONLY CHANCE TO EMBRACE FARTING AND GET TO ENJOY, WITH ALL THE OTHER FARTERS IN THE WORLD, THIS WONDERFUL MEANINGFUL EXPERIENCE .....

NOW, GO FORTH AND MULTIPLY ... THOSE LOVELY FARTS!